anythink

Published in 2017 by Britannica Educational Publishing (a trademark of Encyclopædia Britannica, Inc.) in association with The Rosen Publishing Group, Inc. 29 East 21st Street, New York, NY 10010

Distributed exclusively by Rosen Publishing.
To see additional Britannica Educational Publishing titles, go to rosenpublishing.com
First Edition

Britannica Educational Publishing
J.E. Luebering: Executive Director, Core Editorial
Anthony L. Green: Editor, Compton's by Britannica

Rosen Publishing
Heather Moore Niver: Editor
Nelson Sá: Creative Director
Matt Cauli: Designer
Cindy Reiman: Photography Manager
Heather Moore Niver: Photo Researcher

Library of Congress Cataloging-in-Publication Data

Names: Shea, Therese, author.
Title: Vikings / Therese M. Shea.
Description: New York : Britannica Educational Publishing, [2017] | Series: Warriors around the world | Includes bibliographical references and index.
Identifiers: LCCN 2016021840 | ISBN 9781508103691 (library bound : alk. paper) | ISBN 9781508104308 (pbk. : alk. paper) | ISBN 9781508102960 (6-pack : alk. paper)
Subjects: LCSH: Vikings—Juvenile literature.
Classification: LCC DL66 .S54 2016 | DDC 948/.022—dc23
LC record available at https://lccn.loc.gov/2016021840

Manufactured in China

Photo credits: Cover, p. 3 (Viking) © iStockphoto.com/Khosrork; cover, p. 3 (ship) © iStockphoto.com/ rimglow; cover, p. 3, interior pages (clouds) © iStockphoto.com/Mordolff; p. 7 Bymuseum, Oslo, Norway/Index/Bridgeman Images; p. 11 Philip and Elizabeth De Bay/Corbis Historical/Getty Images; p. 12 © Museumslandschaft Hessen Kassel/Arno Hensmanns/ Bridgeman Images; pp. 13 (inset), 19 Werner Forman/Universal Images Group/Getty Images; pp. 14-15 Windmill Books/ Universal Images Group/Getty Images; pp. 17, 42 Print Collector/Hulton Archive/Getty Images; pp. 20-21 © Richard Peel/ Alamy Stock Photo; pp. 22-23 © Loop Images Ltd/Alamy Stock Photo; p. 25 Encyclopædia Britannica, Inc.; p. 27 Heritage Images/Hulton Archive/Getty Images; p. 29 Popperfoto/Getty Images; p. 30 (inset) Universal History Archive/Universal Images Group/Getty Images; p. 32 De Agostini/Getty Images; p. 33 Kean Collection/Archive Photos/Getty Images; pp. 34-35 AF Archive/Alamy Stock Photo; pp. 36 (inset), 40 Heritage Images/Hulton Fine Art Collection/Getty Images; p. 38 DEA/D. Minassian/De Agostini/Getty Images; p. 39 © imageBROKER/Alamy Stock Photo; interior pages border and background images © iStockphoto.com/LMGPhotos (boats), © iStockphoto.com/freestylephoto (axe), © iStockphoto.com/Dario Lo Presti (shield); © iStockphoto.com/&#169 Nancy Barr-Raper (planks).

CONTENTS

INTRODUCTION

Vikings were seafaring warriors who raided and colonized wide areas of Europe from the ninth to the eleventh centuries, burning, plundering, and killing as they went. These marauders came from Scandinavia—what is now Denmark, Norway, and Sweden. The Vikings were made up of landowning chieftains and clan heads, their followers, freemen, and any energetic young clan members who sought adventure and booty overseas. Some were part-time raiders and pillagers, spending part of the year farming or fishing at home.

Vikings were never a unified group. Rather, the Viking trait of seeking riches outside their homeland was one shared by many peoples who dwelt in Scandinavia. The exact ethnic composition of the Viking armies is unknown in particular cases, but the Vikings' expansion in the Baltic lands and in Russia can probably be attributed to the Swedes. However, the nonmilitary colonization of the Orkney Islands, Faroe Islands, and Iceland was clearly accomplished by the Norwegians.

The Vikings' disruptive influence profoundly affected European history. Their name was given to the era that dated from about 740 CE to about 1050—the Viking Age. During that time, the Scandinavian countries seem to have possessed a practically inexhaustible surplus of manpower. Leaders of ability, who could organize groups of warriors into conquering bands and armies, were seldom

This tenth-century illustration depicts Vikings leaving their ships to explore their fortunes in England. The image was created on vellum, which is parchment made from calfskin.

lacking. These bands would negotiate the seas in their longships and mount hit-and-run raids on cities and towns along the coasts of Europe. Their burning, plundering, and killing earned them the name *vikingr*, meaning "pirate" in the early Scandinavian languages. Their expression for these campaigns of swift, cruel attacks was to "go a-viking."

The fierce reputation of the Viking warrior has survived the centuries. Some attributes are myths, such as their nonexistent horned helmets. However, some truths are more bizarre than anything that could be fabricated, such as the berserkers, the Viking warriors who put themselves in a trance of rage before battle, biting their shields and howling like animals.

Besides warriors, Vikings were artisans, craftsmen, and traders. Vikings were some of the earliest pioneers, trekking across the Atlantic Ocean to Iceland, Greenland, and North America. They traveled throughout Europe and as far east as Central Asia. They exchanged their goods—such as honey, tin, wheat, wool, wood, iron, fur, walrus ivory, and fish—for silver, silk, spices, glass, jewelry, and more. Slaves were also a part of the Viking trade.

Much of our understanding of the Vikings comes from accounts from cultures other than the Scandinavians—often cultures that have been raided or conquered. Some of these biased reports understandably paint Viking warriors as violent, brutal aggressors. The

English cleric and scholar Alcuin the Elder wrote of the Vikings in the late 700s: "Never before has such terror appeared in Britain as we have now suffered from a pagan race." While formidable, the people known as Vikings were a complex civilization who contributed much to European society, even while spreading terror and chaos. Through travels and trade, they helped connect distant cultures, spreading goods as well as ideas.

CHAPTER 1
VIKINGS AT HOME

The word "Viking" has come to be the label applied to the people and culture of Scandinavia during the Viking Age, even those who were not marauders. Vikings more or less looked much like people of today, though perhaps a bit shorter because of poorer nutrition.

BEAUTY AND FASHION

Most cultures have a standard of beauty, and Vikings were no different. Blonde hair was preferred. Men and women used strong soap containing lye to bleach their hair, including the men's beards. Ahmad Ibn Fadlan, a tenth-century Arab traveler, called the Vikings "the filthiest of God's creatures." But at least wealthier Vikings were known for their cleanliness. Tweezers, razors, combs, and ear-cleaning tools made from animal bones and antlers have been found at excavation sites.

Viking men wore jackets and pants. Women wore dresses. Both wore a long cloak fastened at one or both shoulders over their clothes. (Cloaks fashioned over one shoulder made it easier to carry and use a weapon.) Wealthier people wore silver or gold brooches on their cloaks. Shoes were made of calf- or goatskin. Vikings wore skates or spikes on their feet to cross ice-covered surfaces in winter.

This image shows an artist's imagining of Vikings. It is an illustration of a story in which they aid an old Irish woman.

Morris M. Williams

FAMILY TIME

Women married young, as young as twelve years old, but still held some rights, more rights than in many other cultures. They could inherit property, request a divorce, and get their dowry back after a divorce. Historians generally believe women were not soldiers, though some legends relate stories of women warriors called shield maidens.

Viking society was organized by families and clans. Clans lived in villages or towns. Several families often lived together in long wooden houses with thatched roofs. Families worked together to accumulate wealth and protect the interests of the clan. Chieftains were chosen from powerful families to rule over the clan.

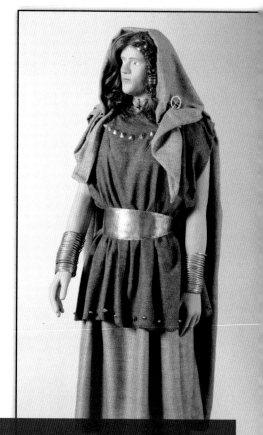

Remnants including articles of clothing found in a grave helped historians dress this model of a Viking woman authentically.

THRALLS, KARLS, JARLS, AND THINGS

The Vikings had a rigid class system. *Thralls* were of the lowest class. They were captured in raids, sentenced to slavery through crimes, or were working to pay off debts. *Thralls* enjoyed few rights even after they were freed.

NORSE MYTHOLOGY

The tales of the early people of Scandinavia are known as Norse mythology. In these myths, Valhalla was the heaven for warriors. The powerful Norse god Odin ruled over it, only allowing warriors who died bravely to go there. Valhalla was a vast banquet hall. Female spirits called Valkyries watched over battlefields. They brought dead heroes to Valhalla. It was said that the dead warriors would enjoy Valhalla until the end of the world. Then they would rise again to fight against evil giants and demons in a final battle called Ragnarök.

This illustration from a fourteenth-century manuscript displays a Swedish king in disguise speaking to the Norse god Odin about the beginning of the world.

13

This drawing of a Viking farmhouse in Iceland is based on archaeological excavations. The roofs of the buildings were made of turf, a dense layer of grass.

Karls were people of the middle class. They were farmers, artisans, traders, and soldiers. Unlike a *thrall*, a *karl* could own land, a mark of true wealth. A *karl* could attain enough wealth, land, and status to become a *jarl*.

Jarls were the most powerful Vikings. They held much land and demanded tribute from people living in their region. *Karls* gave *jarls* support willingly in times of war and foreign expeditions, for *jarls* were the ones who provided ships for trading or raiding parties.

14

A few *jarls* were able to defeat rivals and achieve status as kings.

Scandinavians also had a highly developed legal system, perhaps the most democratic in the world at that time. An assembly called the *thing* allowed the community to reach decisions on matters by voting. All freemen could participate. The *thing* was also a place to settle disputes and try people for crimes. Sometimes two people at odds settled by fighting to the death. Guilty people could also be banished

15

from the community, becoming exiles who by law could be killed on sight.

Such a developed civilization does not correlate with the Viking savage barbarian stereotype. But Viking raiders did not turn to pillaging for arbitrary reasons. Rather, historians believe Danish, Norwegian, and Swedish warriors were probably prompted to undertake raids by a combination of factors including overpopulation at home, a shortage of land, and the helplessness of victims abroad.

INVASION OF IRELAND

Scandinavian invasions of Ireland are recorded from 795, when an island called Rechru was ravaged. Historians think this may have been Rathlin Island off the north coast, which held a monastery at that time. It was looted and set on fire. From then on, fighting was nonstop, and, although the natives often more than held their own, Scandinavian kingdoms arose around the cities of Dublin, Limerick, and Waterford.

Despite victory over the Vikings at the Battle of Clontarf, Irish king Brian Boru was assassinated by Norsemen in 1014.

The kings of Dublin for a time felt strong enough for foreign adventure, and in the early tenth century, several of them ruled in both Dublin and Northumberland. The likelihood that Ireland would be unified under Scandinavian leadership passed with the Battle of Clontarf in 1014. There, the Scandinavians, supported by some Irish, suffered disastrous defeat at the hands of Irish king Brian Boru. The medieval Irish text *The Wars of the Gaedhil with the Gaill* describes what happened when the fleeing Vikings discovered their ships had been carried away by the tide: "They had not at last any place to fly to, but into the sea . . . and the foreigners were drowned in great numbers by the sea, and they lay in heaps and in hundreds."

Yet, the Vikings who had settled there were never truly driven away from Ireland. In the twelfth century, English invaders of Ireland found the Scandinavians still dominant in Dublin, Waterford, Limerick, Wexford, and Cork.

EASTERN EXPANSION

The eastern Viking expansion was probably a less violent process than that on the Atlantic coasts. Although there was, no doubt, plenty of raiding in the Baltic, no Viking kingdom was founded with the sword in that area. Farther south than France—in the Iberian Peninsula and on the Mediterranean coasts— the Vikings raided from time to time but accomplished little of permanence.

Certainly, Viking settlement on the scale of the British Isles was never achieved in the well-defended Carolingian empire (much of modern France, Germany, Switzerland, and Italy under Charlemagne and his successors). Sporadic

The television show Vikings *focuses on famed warrior Ragnar Lothbrok. Here he (*center*) leads a fictional band of warriors ashore during a raid.*

raiding did occur, however, until the end of the Viking period. In 845, Ragnar Lothbrok was said to have sailed his Danish fleet up the Seine River into Paris, France. There, they hung more than one hundred Frankish prisoners as a sacrifice to Odin. The Vikings were offered and accepted 7,000 pounds (3,175 kilograms) of silver to leave.

In the tenth century, settlements on the Seine River became the germ of the duchy of Normandy, the only per-manent Viking achievement in what

THE VARANGIAN GUARD

A further activity of the Scandinavians in the east was in service as mercenaries in Constantinople, the capital of the Byzantine Empire, where they formed the Varangian Guard of the emperor. The first six thousand Vikings were sent by King Vladimir of Russia to his ally. In 988 Emperor Basil II used this force to defeat an army attempting to overthrow him. The Varangian Guard continued to serve as bodyguards and shock troops, those employed in battle for sudden attacks. The Vikings were happy to serve such a wealthy ruler and returned home after their service with extravagant riches.

This illustration from around the twelfth century features the Varangian Guard. It is found in the Madrid Skylitzes, *an illuminated manuscript about the reigns of the Byzantine emperors.*

had been the empire of Charlemagne. Essentially, Normandy was given to the Vikings in exchange for an agreement not to pillage the rest of France.

RAIDING RUSSIA

The greatest eastern movement of the Scandinavians was that which carried them into the heart of Russia. They gave them their name Rus, or "Russians." Although the Scandinavians were at one time dominant in Novgorod, Kiev, and other places, they were rapidly absorbed by the Slavonic population. The Rus were mainly traders. Occasionally, however, the Rus attempted voyages of plunder like their kinsmen in the west. Their existence as a separate people did not continue past 1050 at the latest.

CHAPTER 5
THE LEGACY OF THE VIKINGS

The first half of the eleventh century appears to have seen a new Viking movement toward the east. A number of Swedish runic stones record the names of men who went with Yngvarr the Far-Traveled on his journeys. These journeys were to the east (possibly Persia), but only legendary accounts of their precise direction and intention survive.

IN COMES CHRISTIANITY

The Viking Age ended with the coming of Christianity in Europe. After the eleventh century, the Viking

This rune stone is found in Sweden. Of the seven thousand runic inscriptions worldwide, about half are from the Viking Age.

chief became a figure of the past as did his warriors. Olaf II Haraldsson of Norway, before he became king in 1015, was practically the last Viking chief in the old independent tradition. Denmark became a conquering power, able to absorb the more unruly elements of its population into its royal armies.

Echoes of the Vikings

The Vikings' dominance and reign of terror passed. They settled and assimilated into the many cultures of Europe. However, their mark on history remains.

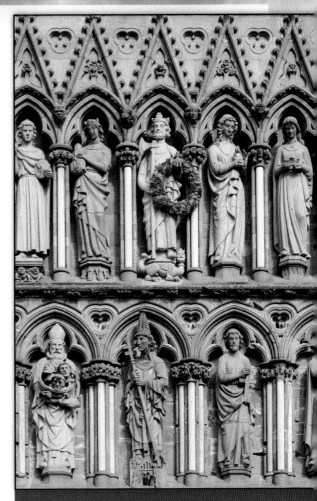

King Olaf II Haraldsson's statue is decorated with a wreath at the Nidaros Cathedral in Trondheim, Norway. He is considered a saint in several religions.

While their exploits became the stuff of legends, the Vikings also had a real influence on European life. Old Norse language is evident in modern English words such as "anger," "bag," "berserk," "dirt," "husband," "knife," "scare," "reindeer," and many, many more. Numerous towns and cities owe their

In this painting by nineteenth-century artist Mårten Eskil Winge, the Norse god Thor wields his mighty hammer to vanquish several giants.

origin to Norse words, including places that end with -*by* ("village" or "settlement") and –*kirk* (from *kirkja* meaning "church"). A number of the days of the week come from Norse gods' names, including Tuesday (from Tiw's Day; Tiw was the god of justice); Wednesday (from Woden's [Odin's] Day); and Thursday (from Thor's Day; Thor was the hammer-carrying god of thunder and lightning).

Another result of Viking warfare was the introduction of taxation in many kingdoms to raise money for defensive structures and armies and to pay tributes and ransoms. Vikings also helped spread currency, which replaced the exchange of goods as the only means of trade. Arab merchants bartered with Vikings using gold

RUNES

The only written monuments of the Vikings themselves are runes, a writing system first developed by Germanic tribes but adopted by Scandinavians. In Sweden, there are some 3,500 inscriptions, mostly written on stone. They were also left in places Viking explorers visited such as Greenland. Some stone monuments feature runes of poetry, while others are thought to be magical spells. A Viking called a rune master was believed to be able to harness the power of magical runes. Runes are also found on Viking swords, pleading with the gods for protection and power during battle.

These coins were discovered in a Viking grave in Sweden dating from the tenth century. Among them are Arab coins, confirming trade between Arabs and Vikings.

and silver coins. In turn, the Vikings used these coins in other places of trade.

DEMYSTIFYING THE VIKINGS

Archaeology is helping to dispel some myths of the Viking culture, aiding in the development of a more realistic and balanced picture of these people. Today, it is possible to visit reconstructed Viking villages to understand more about how these people may have lived. Birka, Sweden, an early trading center, boasts a re-created Viking harbor and Scandinavia's largest Viking cemetery, including about three thousand graves.

Because Vikings did not keep their own records, their depiction from the point of view of the people they encountered is their lasting reputation. They were undoubtedly aggressive and violent at times, but probably no more than other contemporary peoples. While fierce warriors, they were also artisans, shipbuilders, farmers, and explorers. Both facts and fiction will help keep modern people fascinated by the extraordinary people called Vikings.

GLOSSARY

arbitrary Not planned or chosen for a particular reason.

assimilate To fully become part of a different society.

berserk Crazy and violent, especially because of anger.

cavalry The part of an army that in the past had soldiers who rode horses.

Celt A member of a group of people who lived mostly in ancient Britain and parts of western Europe.

chainmail A kind of protective clothing that is made up of tiny metal rings that are linked together and that was worn by knights and soldiers in the Middle Ages.

dowry Money or property that a wife or wife's family gives to her husband when the wife and husband marry in some cultures.

duchy An area of land that is controlled by a duke or duchess.

excavation The action of uncovering something by digging away and removing the earth that covers it.

maneuver A planned movement of soldiers.

marauder One who roams about and raids in search of things to steal.

pagan A follower of a religion of many gods.

plunder To steal things from a place, especially by force.

prow The front of a ship.

ransom Money that is paid in order to free someone who has been captured or kidnapped.

ravage To commit destructive actions.

retinue A group of helpers, supporters, or followers.

rivet A special kind of metal bolt or pin that is used to hold pieces of metal together.

siege A military blockade of a city or fortified place to compel it to surrender.

sporadic Occurring occasionally.

tactics The activity or skill of organizing and moving soldiers and equipment in a military battle.

thatched Having a roof made of dried plants.

trance A sleeplike state in which one can move and respond.

tribute Money or goods that a ruler or country gives to another ruler or country, especially for protection.

FOR FURTHER READING

Castleden, Rodney. *Vikings: Warriors, Traders, and Masters of the Sea.* New York, NY: Chartwell Books, 2015.

Cooke, Tim. *The Vikings.* Tucson, AZ: Brown Bear Books Ltd., 2014.

Dillard, Sheri. *Viking Warriors.* Mankato, MN: Child's World, 2015.

Ganeri, Anita. *How to Live Like a Viking Warrior.* Minneapolis, MN: Hungry Tomato, 2015.

Harman, Alice. *The Vikings.* London, UK: Wayland, 2014.

Lee, Adrienne. *Vikings.* North Mankato, MN: Capstone Press, 2014.

Linskey, Howard. *Vikings.* Stevenage, UK: Badger Learning, 2014.

Manning, Mick, and Brita Granström. *Viking Longship.* London, UK: Frances Lincoln Children's Books, 2015.

Steele, Philip. *Vikings.* New York, NY: Kingfisher, 2014.

WEBSITES

Because of the changing nature of internet links, Rosen Publishing has developed an online list of websites related to the subject of this book. This site is updated regularly. Please use this link to access this list:

http://www.rosenlinks.com/WAW/viking

INDEX

A
Alfred, King, 26, 28
armor, 18
Athelstan, King, 28

B
banishment/exile, 15–16, 20
berserkers, 8, 22
Birka, Sweden, 43
blonde hair, 10
Brunaburh, Battle of, 28

C
chieftain, 6, 12, 18, 20, 39
Christianity, 30, 38–39
clans, 6, 12
Clontarf, Battle of, 33
clothing, 10
currency, 41, 43

D
Danelaw, 28

E
Eddington, Battle of, 28

H
helmets, 8, 18
hirds, 18, 20
housing, 12
hygiene, 10

J
jarls, 14, 15, 30

K
karls, 14

L
Lindisfarne, 25
longships, 22–24
long sword, 17
Lothbrok, Ragnar, 26, 35

N
Norse
   mythology, 13
   words used today, 39, 41

O
Odin, 13, 22, 35, 41